# TRAVELLING TO ABSURDISTAN

## CURIOUS STORIES ON THE ROAD

### BY ANNA ZOCH

# Travelling to Absurdistan

## Curious Stories on the Road

## by Anna Zoch

Bibliographic information from the German National Library:

The German National Library lists this publication in the German National Bibliography; detailed bibliographic data is available on the Internet at http://dnb.dnb.de.

Text und photos: Anna Zoch (photo p. 131: couple Dünchem)

Manufacture and publishing: BoD – Books on Demand, Norderstedt

ISBN:  978 3754 304648

# Index

# 1. Preface

„If someone goes on a trip, he has something to talk about!"

This is all the more true for me, as I have been traveling as a study tour guide for many years, mainly in north-western Europe.

Anyone who works with people knows that it is never boring. Our fellow human beings always cause unforeseen and sometimes very curious situations. In my long-term work, I have now seen numerous events, some of them quite absurd.

At some point, I started to write my stories down in order to be able to remember these special trips and, above all else, my many guests. Each anecdote stands for itself. Sometimes, however, experiences from several journeys have merged into one story.

The "common thread" of all stories is my great love and passion for my job as tour guide.

I wish to share these personal moments and experiences with you now and invite you on an exclusive trip to my private "Absurdistan"!

Would you like to join me?

**In front of the Admiralty Church in Karlskrona with "Mats Rosenboom", known from the novel "Nils Holgersson" by Selma Lagerlöf**

## 2. "My Swedish Suitcase Thriller"

A summer in Sweden! Who doesn't immediately think of a bright blue sky with puffy clouds, of the countless lakes or the sound of the surf, of red wooden houses on bare archipelago cliffs polished smooth by the ice, of a true summer idyll in the country or at the coast, strawberries with cream, in white clad, and blond and partying Swedes! And everything in a calm and relaxation mood, the hectic rush and stress seem far away ... Oh yes, that is the Swedish summer, definitely, I've seen it again and again, so very exciting.

But, this idyllic impression can also be deceptive. Do not trust the "Lindström" certificate so lightly: We are on our way in Sweden, a country where the grotesque, absurd and even criminal can happen. You don't want to believe it? Then I will tell you about my personal suitcase thriller, which also happened in the very tranquil southern Sweden.

When I started my first one-week tour of Sweden in the 2012 summer season, I had no inkling of what was going to happen. Full of joyful anticipation, I arrive from Hamburg Airport with my guests from Germany, Austria and

Switzerland. We fly to Jönköping, which is picturesquely located on the south bank of Lake Vättern. After landing at the small airport, all passengers walk across the tarmac to the terminal. This walk alone, coupled with the sight of the small, automatic lawnmowers, which do their rounds in front of the terminal building, trigger astonishment and budding enthusiasm among the passengers.

Then the wait at the luggage belt, where the first pieces of luggage will soon appear. Those who receive their suitcases can consider themselves lucky, because I quickly realize that this is not a given situation.

Connection flights, in particular, seem to carry with them the innate risk that reloading and forwarding of the suitcase is not always guaranteed. So, one of my first official acts at the airport is to submit the "missing person report" of two suitcases, the owners are a slightly angry mother-daughter team. "This is a great way to start your vacation!" is their sarcastic comment, which I should hear more often … to my deepest regret.

Soon afterwards, rain sets in - greetings from "Murphy"! The rain jackets of my suitcaseless guests are of course well and safely stowed in their suitcases. We spend our first night in Jönköping, but unfortunately, it is not possible to shop for cosmetics that day. Because it is midsummer and all the shops are closed, but luckily, our hotel is prepared for such emergencies.

The next day, a Sunday, takes us south-west to Lund in Skåne, where we will spend the second night. In the course of the evening, one of the missing suitcases actually arrives, but one is still missing, although the two "injured parties" did traveled together. In the meantime, the nerves of the guest, whose suitcase is still on the move, and who has spent the whole day at around 18°C without a jacket while encountering several rain showers, are pretty fried. The next morning there is the redemption: shortly before our departure from Lund in the direction of Malmö, a taxi from Copenhagen Airport arrives at the hotel with the last missing suitcase! The rest of the trip runs without further losses worth mentioning, and in the end, it is a wonderful travel experience in the Midsummer Night's Dream for all guests, despite the initial obstacles.

The next summer I am flying back to Sweden, full of anticipation and cheerfulness, not knowing that this time the suitcase drama will increase. After the first two weeks of successful and problem-free tours, the arrival of the third group of guests leads to a "meltdown"! The suitcases of 10 passengers are missing, this is almost a third of my group, and all from different departure airports: Vienna, Zurich, Munich, Frankfurt and Düsseldorf. This cannot be true! A colleague, with a completely different travel program, also has lost luggage. Initially, the procedure is the same as the past year's. Again, the losses have to be reported. But, in the meantime, I copy the list with the respective hotels and my Swedish mobile phone number as a precaution and I leave it at the airport in Jönköping.

This time it, the arrival is on a normal weekend so that the most urgent items can be bought in Jönköping. Of course, none of those affected are enthusiastic, especially a gentleman from Austria reacts very indignantly about his loss of a suitcase and, in addition, believes that he got a particularly bad hotel room. This is when it is really necessary to have a light touch ... Again a journey begins under poor starting conditions, again I hear the sarcastic sentence "This is a great way to start a vacation!" But at least this time the weather holds.

Hoping that at least some of the missing luggage might be in Lund the following evening, we set off the next morning. Halfway to our first stop of the program my cell phone rings. Somebody from Copenhagen Airport wants to know the reference numbers of the injured parties, which are listed on their receipts. I ask for a call back at a later time, because their phone number is not visible on my display and after all, I still have to complete my program, so I cannot always make calls. After the visit at our next stop, all those affected look for the required paper in their existing luggage.

Then we drive on and I hope to be called back at the next stop in order to provide the requested information. The callback comes, as I somehow suspected, shortly after our next departure, again at an inconvenient time. So I ask them to call me back during our next stop, not considering that there is hardly any cell phone reception in the headland on Kullaberg! And of course, the requested callback only arrives at our departure.

The next destination is Lund, the location of our hotel for this night and not too far from the

Copenhagen and Malmö airports. Our hopes of finding the missing suitcase on arrival at the hotel is quickly dashed, but the evening is still ahead of us and the missing luggage could still arrive before we leave for Malmö the next morning. Then we go to bed and dream of suitcases... Yes, me too, because I received another call that evening. This time it is the airport in Malmö with the good news that the missing luggage would arrive there the next morning around 11 a.m. Unfortunately, that is about the same time as our departure time for the next stop on the trip, which is about two hours from Malmö. The disappointment of a third of the guests that their suitcases did not arrive for breakfast is not particularly conducive to a group trip. So, what shall I do? I decide to detour our trip past Malmö Airport, even if this delays the rest of the day's program. After all, a large part of the tour group is affected.

We drive to Malmö Airport, which is in the exact opposite direction of our program, and arrive full of hope. And thankfully, various abandoned suitcases are found in the terminal. But, three of the missing bags are still lost. I console my grumbling and now unfortunately slightly smelly guests, after all, there is also an airport in Kalmar, where we find our next hotel. Additionally, there is shopping in Karlskrona that afternoon, but the weather is just too nice! Sincerely, these are not really particularly good moments in the life of a tour guide...

On the way, I get a call from Kalmar airport: our missing suitcases are on their way and will be taken to the hotel in a taxi. Hallelujah what a joy! When we reach the hotel in Kalmar in the evening, a taxi actually pulls up and delivers TWO of the three missing suitcases. The person concerned, a lovely professor from Zurich, now loses his composure and explains to me that he has been walking around in the same clothes for three days and that this situation is no longer bearable for him and his fellow travelers in view of the summer temperatures. ... His suitcase will arrive in the course of the next evening in Stockholm, by which we have already completed half of our trip.

That evening, the following happened at the hotel in Stockholm. I received a call from Stockholm International Airport in Arlanda saying that the last remaining suitcase will be delivered to the hotel. Shortly before 11 p.m., the last suitcase has already arrived, my mobile phone rings again: this time it is the hotel reception. A suitcase has arrived and names from my travel group are written on the banderole. I go downstairs and I am stumped at the names on the banderole: there is a total of three names and two match guests from my group. BUT we already have all of our luggage and I don't know what to do with this excess suitcase! So I tell the receptionist to send this suitcase back since we have already been taken care of! That week, I get the impression that my Swedish mobile number is on file at all the airports and that I am the first contact person for all "abandoned" suitcases during that time. In the end, the mess was never completely explained. Hamburg Airport probably misdirected a complete suitcase trolley.

With these experiences in mind, I start the next summer season one year later and this time I will be the victim! I however will not see my suitcase ever again; it will be a permanent disappearance and an involuntary meeting with the colleagues of "Detective Wallander".

After three days with a full program, we arrive in the late afternoon and a bit delayed, at our hotel in the old town of Malmö, which you can only reach on foot. We are a small group in a Sprinter bus, pulling a trailer for the suitcases. Because it is already late, I leave my bag with documents in the bus and only take the small bag with my luggage for the night. My big suitcase stays in the trailer! A mistake, as it will sadly turn out. The evening began with such great anticipation: since it is the final of the soccer World Cup! However, it drags on and Germany only wins against Argentina in over time. While I am hoping for a quick end after a long day, I get a call from my driver. Our bus was broken into and my briefcase and suitcase are gone! This is a big shock for me: the loss of my clothing is one thing, the loss of my documents is much worse...

Thankfully, the next morning the wonderful news arrives that someone has found my briefcase in the Central Park of Malmö not far from the hotel and was able to contact my driver based on the documents found inside: I get almost everything back! I am very relieved. However, we have to report the bus break-in and theft. At the next opportunity, I go to the police to report my loss where I hear the word "semester" - the Swedish word for vacation - several times from these friendly officers! I now realize that I can write my suitcase off. And that is how it was! To this day I have no information about the whereabouts or rather the disappearance of my suitcase.

During my trip with two-overnight-stays in Malmö in 2019, before we arrive, I tell my guests about this past experiences and emphasize that since then, I have never left bags, documents or any other important items in the bus, not even in the smallest provincial towns in Sweden! The next morning, about 30 minutes before our agreed departure time, I meet a completely distraught and shocked bus driver who tells me that our bus has been broken into. Strange but true! And so that day, a Sunday, I have the dubious "pleasure" of contacting the local police, again. Incomprehensibly however, despite my urgent warning, a guest left his mobile phone in the bus, which of course was never to be seen again.

I am a big fan of Swedish crime novels. But, my personal experience made it clear, that caution is advisable in this supposedly idyllic country. Unfortunately, detective Wallander and his colleagues have a sad "right to exist".

Perhaps it is precisely the contrast between idyllic "Bullerbü Sweden" and the reality that makes Swedish crime novels so successful...

**View of Södermalm in Stockholm**

**View from Malmö to the Oresund Bridge**

## 3. "My Night with Queen Silvia"

„Why do you have all these barriers here in the parking lot? And why is there police parked in front of the hotel? Who is arriving today?" I ask the police officers in front of the castle hotel in Gotha on April 7th, 2014. My next question is more practical: "Where shall we park our bus today?"

I am traveling with guests in Thuringia on the trail of the titans of German history: Luther, Goethe, Schiller and Bach. We stay in the castle hotel in Gotha adjacent to the castle's park and went on an excursion to Erfurt, Weimar, Arnstadt and the Wartburg. But, when we return, the hotel parking lot is blocked, and a large police presence in front of the hotel regulates traffic.

"Today, Queen Silvia of Sweden will be presented with a prize at the Friedenstein Castle in Gotha and she will spend the night here," said the friendly police officer, who then explained further where to park the bus that night.

I can hardly stop myself in my excitement! Queen Silvia of Sweden and I will spend the night under one roof! Of course, I want to take photos as proof of this unique and once in a lifetime encounter, and so I go on a discovery tour. At the reception, as expected, my pursuit is discouraged with these unhelpful words: "We are not permitted to give out any information about her itinerary!"

However, I find out that the first floor of the hotel will be completely royal for the next night and so I just go to have a look. It is unbelievable! Nobody stops me! I even talk to one of the security guards, who tells me the program for the following day: planned is an early morning walk in the park in the direction of the castle, followed by an official farewell in front of the hotel.

That evening in front of the hotel, together with a few other photographers, I lie in wait for a nice photo, but the whole thing passes by just too fast! Queen Silvia comes out of the hotel, gets into the limousine and is off to her evening program. Just a second too late, I press the shutter release of my camera. But there is still a chance the next day! And I definitely don't want to miss that. So, early in the morning, I visit the park across from the hotel full of anticipation. Queen Silvia is supposed to take a morning stroll in the direction of the castle ... and amazingly, after I hold out for a long while on my park bench, she arrives with her lady-in-waiting, the royal press officer and some security guards.

I shoot some photos from a distance, but out of respect, hold back when she comes closer. Such a "close encounter" with a queen, will probably never again be in my cards. She walks right past me! I am very happy with my loot of photos.

Shortly afterwards her limousine pulls up in front of the hotel and Queen Silvia is officially bidden farewell by the city officials. My guests and I find a spot only ca. 10 meters from this action and Queen Silvia even greets us! What a special occasion for all of us. Because who can truly say: "We spent a night with Queen Silvia!"

**Farewell in front of the castle hotel in Gotha**

And now it's a beautiful story for me ...

### *More about Queen Silvia ...*

*Silvia Renate Sommerlath was born on the 23$^{rd}$ of December, 1943 in Heidelberg as the daughter of Walther Sommerlath and his Brazilian born wife Alice Soares de Toledo. Between 1947 and 1957, she was raised in São Paulo. In 1957, the family returned to Germany. In 1963, she graduated high school at the Luisen-Gymnasium in Düsseldorf; from 1965 to 1969, she attended the Language and Interpreting Institute in Munich. Next to Swedish and German, she speaks French, Spanish,*

*Portuguese, English, and the Swedish sign language. She worked in the Argentinian consulate in Munich, as hostess for the 1972 Summer Olympics in Munich, and as deputy chief of protocol for the 1976 Winter Olympics in Innsbruck.*

*Silvia Sommerlath made the acquaintance of her future husband, Carl XVI, as hostess at the 1972 Summer Olympics in Munich. She married Gustaf of Sweden on June 19$^{th}$, 1976 in Stockholm's Storkyrka. The day before their engagement, on March 12$^{th}$, 1976, the Swedish pop group ABBA premiered their song "Dancing Queen" on Swedish TV in honor of the royal couple to be.*

*In addition to her royal duties, Silvia is a spokesperson for disadvantaged and abused children. In 1999, she founded the World Childhood Foundation. Even earlier, in 1990, she received the German Culture Prize for her commitment for para sports; in 2002, she received the German Media Prize in Baden-Baden and in 2006 the Honorary Bambi from the publishing house Hubert Burda Media. Queen Silvia is the patron of the grand sum of 62 associations. Near the Drottningholm Palace, Silvia founded the Silviahemmet (Swedish for "The Silvia Home"), where people with dementia are cared for. In addition, the royal couple also established the Royal Wedding Fund, which supports research in the field of para sports.*

*In Gotha, Queen Silvia of Sweden was honored for her life's work and her commitment to children. The Heidelberg born received the "Peace Stone" award in the castle with the same name. Queen Silvia's husband, King Carl XVI, Gustaf of Sweden is related to the ducal houses of Saxe-Coburg and Gotha.*

## 4. "Sensational Find in Rannoch Moor"

In the autumn of 2016, I leave on a wonderful trip into the heart of Scotland; our destination is the picturesque little town of Pitlochry, about half an hour's drive on the A9 north of Perth. One of our excursions takes us to Rannoch Moor, an area of around 130 km² that is considered to be one of the last untouched regions of Scotland. The area is characterized as countless peat swamps, watercourses, ponds, and lakes, as well as a watershed: the lakes and rivers to the west drain into the Atlantic Ocean, the eastern waters flow into the River Tay and from there into the North

Sea. At the Victorian train station, the Rannoch Station, we plan to have a lunchtime picnic with Scottish specialties.

The small train station is far off the usual tourist routes. To make our way there, we first take the B8019 near Pitlochry. Soon we reach the wonderful viewpoint "Queen's View" with a direct sight of Loch Tummel, and which Queen Victoria is said to have enjoyed in the 19th century. Following the road, we continue through Tay Forest Park and along Loch Rannoch. We pass countless meadows with sheep, see ancient, massive trees covered with lichen and the typically Scottish Highland Cattle.

Most of the vehicles of the oncoming traffic are forestry trucks. Such an encounter on a "single road track", a single-lane road with passing bays, is always exciting. The drivers must then maneuver with millimeter precision.

At the end of the street, we see a sign indicating a dead end. We reach a lunar landscape with barren hills, covered only with heather and grass. Completely unexpectedly, a small settlement appears at the end of the road. There is even a hotel. In the small train station from 1894, thirsty train passengers find a cozy "tea room". The trains run either towards Glasgow or Fort William. Many hikers strengthen themselves once more before making their way through the high moor into the legendary GlenCoe valley.[1]

---

[1] In February 1692, a perfidious massacre of the local MacDonalds clan occurred, which earned the valley the nickname "the Valley of Tears". The 1688 appointed King William III of Orange (the Protestant son-in-law of the deposed Stuart James VII.) demanded of all the highland chiefs to take an oath of allegiance, which was to be sworn by 1691. Alistair MacDonald of GlenCoe hesitated for a long time, then was delayed due to the winter weather and thus a terrible example was made of his clan. Unthinkably, the neighboring Campbells, with whom the MacDonalds were at odds, were charged with this terrible bloody act. They enjoyed the MacDonald's hospitality for about two weeks. This was considered the highest honor in the Highlands and was also granted to members of a warring clan. The royal order entailed "to spare no man under the age of 70!" Many fled to the mountains and froze to death. All of Europe was shocked by the abuse of hospitality but not by the slaughter of the Scots among themselves, since this was nothing new. To this day, the traditional song "The massacre of GlenCoe" commemorates this event, and members of the Campbell clan were denied access to GlenCoe until the 1970s!

After our picnic at the train station, I go for a short walk. After just a few meters, I stop in surprise in front of a weathered wood root covered in moss, which immediately inspires my imagination.

This looks a whole lot like "Nessie", I think immediately ... but I know all the "Nessies" from Loch Ness, yet this one is completely different and I am very excited! I immediately take photos for evidence.

My incredible discovery in Rannoch Moor and my proof inspire me to write an exciting story for the tabloid press. I can already see the following headline in my mind's eye:

**"News from the Summer Holidays: Nessie is on vacation!** Sensational discovery! "Nessie" is in Rannoch Moor! Why there? In this barren loneliness? With Fort William in the north, Tyndrum in the south, the legendary GlenCoe in the west? Quite simple: "Nessie" is on vacation! Absolutely understandable, so shortly after the main holiday season. Way too much stress for "Nessie"! Daily visitors from all over the world at Loch Ness! Everyone wants an exclusive photo opportunity! "Nessie" had enough! Away on vacation! Very far away, where nobody would expect "Nessie"!"

That would be another unbelievable story to complement the many historic reports on "Nessie". But why should the Loch Ness Monster choose Rannoch Moor as a holiday retreat? Well, it is quite obvious to me: peace and relaxation are guaranteed here and, in addition, it would be quite easy for "Nessie" to get there.

From Loch Ness it goes first through the Caledonian Canal. This channel was created at the beginning of the 19th century as an artificial waterway that connects the lochs (lakes) in the Great Glen, the large valley. This enabled merchant ships to travel right through the country. With the construction of the railway lines shortly afterwards, this canal very quickly lost its original economic importance and is now only frequented by "leisure captains". Continuing through Loch Oich and Loch Lochy, "Nessie" can easily and comfortably reach Fort William by water, and from there the journey continues via train in the direction of Glasgow to Rannoch Moor. This is how I imagine the travel route...

A trip to Scotland without a visit to Loch Ness is certainly possible, but for most visitors it is unthinkable. At least not for those visiting Scotland for the first time or even just once. Many visitors from around the world come to Loch Ness each year and visit Urqhart Castle, which is located on a peninsula about 30 km south of Inverness. The birth of today's castle ruins can be found in the 13th century. In the centuries that followed, the castle was expanded into an imposing complex and blown up in the 17th century. Since then, the picturesque ruin has attracted countless guests from all over the world, including the Nation's poets of Scotland Robert Burns and Theodor Fontane...

**View from Urqhart Castle over Loch Ness**

This is also said to be the best place to search for "Nessie". No wonder that in the high season, from May to September, tongs of visitors line up in front of the castle to search for the mysterious "snake" ☺...

Today, there are innumerable references to the legendary monster of Scotland, the first going back to the 6th century! It is said to have been Saint Columba, an Irish missionary, who in 563 AD founded the monastery of Iona on the west coast of Scotland. From there he brought the Christian faith to the Picts, the indigenous people of Scotland, and is said to have seen a water monster on the River Ness. One of his monks was attacked while crossing the river. Columba made the sign of the cross and shouted: "Do not go any further and do not touch that man. Quick! Withdraw!" Whereupon the monster is said to have disappeared.

With the construction of the A82 roadway from Fort Williams to Inverness in the early 1930s, the first modern observations were made by honorable and credible people, such as the directress of the Drumnadrochit Hotel. This triggered a real boom! Countless "evidence photos" were circulating in the press. The best known of these dates from 1934 and was only proved fake in 1994. A big game hunter with a good sense of humor presented the British Museum with a plaster cast that he had made using a hippopotamus ashtray. Since then, Loch Ness has been explored with sometimes quite elaborate means and attempts are being made to fathom the secret of "Nessie". Researchers lay in wait with special cameras, a submarine was also deployed, and even a special sonar ship was built in the 1980s.

To this day, Loch Ness holds many secrets; the largest lake in Great Britain is currently not fully explored. The reports of its depth varies considerably, between over 200 meters to more than 300 meters. Allegedly, there is room for three times the volume of humanity in Loch Ness. Floating particles in the water significantly restricts the view under water; additionally there is the year-round constant water temperature of around 6 to 8°C.

A theory of "Nessie research" states that a marine dinosaur may have survived the passage of time in Loch Ness; the discovery of the coelacanth in 1938 and 1997, which was considered to be extinct, speaks for this possibility! After the last ice age, due to the rising of the land, Loch Ness became an inland lake; previously it was a bay of the North Sea. Did a group of marine dinosaurs survive there? Loch Ness is said to be very rich in fish, so there would be enough food ... but what about the carcasses and corpses that cannot be found? Is this food for Nessie? When one of my guests showed up with a considerable delay at the bus, a correlated rumor had already circulated among the guests that this missing person was most certainly the latest "victim of Nessie" ...

Hopefully the mystery will remain, even if the BBC announcement from 05.09.2019 deliver a new sober explanation: "The Loch Ness Monster could be a gigantic eel!"

https://www.bbc.com/news/uk-scotland-highlands-islands-49495145

In any case, the whole region has been living off the mystery "Nessie" for many years. Leaving the city of Inverness, the visitor travels on the "Nessie Trail"; in the town of Drumnadrochit he can delve into the subject in both the "Nessieland" as well as in the "Loch Ness Experience". During a tour, the visitor is informed at several stations about Loch Ness and the "scientific research" about the legendary monster. In the outdoor area, you can even see the submarine that was once supposed to reveal the secret. And of course "Nessie" is also present!

Scotland is also known for the cloned sheep "Dollie", why shouldn't "Nessie" also be cloned? That at least would explain why there are four "Nessies", including two "Baby-Nessies", to be found alone in the small town of Drumnadrochit. Of course, not to be forgotten, the "Nessie" in front of the Clansman Harbor Hotel. Boat trips to Urqhart Castle start from there. The boat journeys in a wide arch around the ruin and then docks at the pier. The waves can be seen for a long time after the boat has disappeared from the observer's field of vision. And if the visitor goes on to the town of Fort Augustus at the south end of Loch Ness, he will encounter another "Nessie" at the lock steps of the Caledonian Canal. This one is a version made of metal wires. This offers the tourists from all over the world many different photo opportunities around Loch Ness. Certainly, nobody can ever say that they have not seen "Nessie" after visiting!

What surprises me, however, is the fact that "Nessie" has not yet been included in the official canon of Scottish music. But good things come to those who wait. Then maybe at some point we will not only hear something about the "Bonnie, Bonnie banks of Loch Lomond", but also something about "Bonnie, Bonnie Nessie, the secret of Loch Ness"! For most visitors today, "Nessie" is part of their trip to Scotland just like whiskey, sheep, kilts and bagpipes!

By the way: I have met "Nessie" again and again in the coming years near the train station in Rannoch Moor, always at the beginning of September! That cannot be a coincidence! So, if you are looking for a really exclusive encounter with "Nessie", I recommend a visit to Rannoch Moor Station! Be it to meet "Nessie", to drink tea, to start your hike through the moor or to take the train...

**My "sensational photo" in Rannoch Moor!**

**And here one from "Nessie" in Dumnadrochit...**

## 5. "With 49 Adventurers in Scotland"

I am very excited about my first touring trip in Scotland this year and thus also about my season opener in the northern parts of the British Isles, which I so dearly love. I am sitting on the plane to Scotland in the middle of May and have no idea what will be in store for me these next few days. Scotland is my absolute favorite country; however, this sentiment will be put to the test in the days to come.

In the evening, I introduce myself to my guests as the ghost of the hotel since, officially, I am not even on duty yet. They have arrived, throughout the day, from all over Germany and Austria.

Officially, I do not start work until the next morning and I bid them goodnight with some essential survival tips for their first Scottish meal.

It is customary in Great Britain for guests to combine their own dinner: they choose one of two to three starters, as well as from an equal number of main courses and desserts, and thus create their own individual menu.

The next morning, all guests appear healthy and eagerly awaiting the start of the trip. But, our bus is a long time coming. Finally, he arrives delayed and while loading the luggage and the guests we experience the first moment of conflict on this tour. A gentleman, from the Austrian country side, angrily shoves an official document from Heathrow airport under my nose. His explanation, given in a dialect brawl, that is almost incomprehensible to me, since I stem from northern Germany and speak purely high, printable German. The document turns out to be a missing person's report for his suitcase! I think "Oh no", because I intently remember my previous experiences with missing luggage. I only know too well from previous years how long a search for a missing suitcase can take.

But now we finally have to get going! Our 15-minute delay may not seem so dramatic at first, but it has a domino effect on all of the next items on the day's program, which should not be underestimated!

Stowing the entire luggage is a first logistical challenge for our driver. Why some guests travel with luggage for a week-long trip, that would be appropriate for a trip around the world, is still not comprehensible to me. "You have to be prepared for anything; you never know what the weather will be". Well, this is true, especially in Scotland you should be prepared for almost any seasons in terms of weather. Nevertheless, Scotland is not a country in which missing clothing cannot be bought and that at very reasonable prices.

At the beginning of a journey there is hardly any solidarity between fellow travelers: "If I can't sit with my wife, we'll break off the trip!" one guest informed me indignantly. This statement strains my good upbringing so much so I do not see the availability of two free seats in the moment and calm the seas with my guest: "Please all get in first, we will find a solution!" That is my Go-To (and most likely not just mine!) to get going first and foremost. What comes afterwards, we will see...

### Now 49 guests are sitting in a bus with 49 seats!

Three of my guests are traveling as singles and thus inadvertently become a major logistical challenge for all other fellow travelers. And at this point in time I cannot imagine how this will cause a real trial for everyone on the bus.

Late noon we complete our city tour through Edinburgh with many wonderful impressions and, after some free time in the center of the capital of

Scotland, we continue on to Tyndrum to find our next hotel.

The first opportunity to solve the seat problem quickly passed. One of the missing guests traveling alone shows up with some delay at the agreed upon meeting point. At departure, I count 49 guests on 49 seats, but why am I still counting? After all, "only" all the seats have to be occupied.

My phone call that afternoon with the responsible travel agency got me the somewhat succinct information that it is high season right now (You think!) and that therefore no other bus was available. In addition, the "seat occupancy" is perfect from a commercial point of view! Thank you very much for this information! Even my call to British Airways about the missing suitcase only raises questions that I cannot answer in that moment.

After checking in at the hotel, where we will be staying the next three nights, some of my fellow travelers have a first conspiratorial meeting with me in order to find a well-meaning solution to the seating problem: "Whoever shows up first the next morning finds themselves their place!". A great suggestion! Unfortunately, however, it completely misses the notion of most of the other travelers! For them, the rule generally applies: "This is my seat, I fought for it on the first day of the trip at the risk of my own life and I will defend it until the end of the trip! - After all, I have already deposited my rain jacket and my Sudoku book here." Unreasonable to change this again this late.

A typical "towel mentality" is expressed by an alarmingly high number of guests, but here in relation to the seats on the bus. Unfortunately, there always happen to be guests who get sick if they cannot sit in the two front rows of the bus. It is striking that this malady often plagues passionate photographers! I also have such a "case" among my guests. And it is also one of the solo travelers and, according to her, there is no way that a seat in the back of the bus will do! Well, this makes me really look forward to the next morning: The "slashing and stabbing" will definitely go into the next round! However now, first let's get dinner: Cheers and Goodnight!

The next morning, after the battle at the breakfast buffet, I make my way to the bus in the safe expectation of another seat discussion, which arrives promptly. One of my guests comes to me with the complaint that the lady in question has "taken his seat" next to his wife. The latter, in turn, vehemently insists on her position that she cannot sit in the back of the bus, this would make her sick - my stomach also suddenly feels a little queasy! Should this unruly discussion be repeated every morning? In this instant, I ask the husband to take that unpopular middle seat in the last row, because we have to get to a ferry on time and therefore we must leave at once.

**Tobermory harbor**

Our destination for the day is Tobermory on the Hebridean island of Mull. We start the trip first to Oban, with approx. 8000 inhabitants the largest city in the region and characterized by its port. From here, the ferries leave for the Inner

Hebrides, a group of islands on the west coast of Scotland. After a 45-minute ferry ride and an hour by bus, we arrive in Tobermory, the main town of the island. Visitor can find here a small whiskey distillery right by the harbor. But above all else, the many colorful houses define the picturesque local scenery.

After this stop with the opportunity to eat fish and chips, we return to the Scottish mainland, with free time for the guests in the port city of Oban. The city is overshadowed by an incomplete replica of the Colosseum: McCaig's Tower. This is characteristic of the Scottish mentality. A really crazy idea, which the once wealthy banker John Stuart McCaig had, which also started as a job creation scheme for this town. But, the money ran out before completion and thus today this unfinished family memorial has become a popular vantage point with a fantastic view of the harbor and the promenade. So, with another day's program in the bag, I am truly excited. Is there a seal in that harbor basin? How cute...

The next day starts harmlessly, but the crazy weather will put a spoke in our wheel! But to begin however, the day's program is optimized.

In order not to have to drive the same route thrice, we reverse the program. In the morning, we initially follow the extremely serpentine route of the A82 along the northern end of Loch Lomond. From there, we travel to Inveraray and on our drive back there is a surprise photo stop at Kilchurn Castle, before we return to the hotel in Tyndrum. Everything is going well, the weather cooperates, and the guests are very satisfied and happy about the stop at Kilchurn Castle, a picturesque ruin and a popular photo motive. Just another 30-minutes-drive and we would be back at the hotel ... then we reach the next intersection: a police car! We cannot go any further; the road is closed due to a field fire, which has to be extinguished with the help of helicopters! This means for us: We have to drive all the way back, an additional journey of around two hours at the end of a long and beautiful day. Now solidarity is required, biscuits and bananas are thrown in the mix, the only slightly annoyed objection of a guest according to the motto: "That's really great!" is deliberately overheard by all other guests and drowned out with loud Scottish music! We return to the hotel a little exhausted, but as a tight knit community. That evening the hotel bar shows a remarkably good turnover!

The next morning the fight for the most coveted seats repeats itself: The "problematic" lady has again taken a seat without consultation that is convenient for her and feels completely within her rights! This time the single male comes to me and demands a clear verdict from me on the matter. I should take control now! However, for me, at this moment, and much more stomach turning is the fact that our ferry connection from Mallaig to the Isle of Skye will not take place: because the only ferry that could transport this bus is in the workshop! And my dear "sheep" do not even know yet that this fact means additional travel of several hours, which will then shorten our stay on the "island of fog" considerably. Following the motto: "How do I tell my child?" in the back of my mind, we leave through the wonderfully beautiful GlenCoe that morning in glorious Scottish rain. I tell the dramatic story of the massacre committed by the Campbell clan on the MacDonalds in 1692, which has earned the valley the nickname "Valley of Tears". We make our mandatory photo stop and see a rainbow! Well, if this isn't nice! Yet again, the Scottish proverb runs true: "You don't like the weather, then wait a few minutes!" The next stop in the program is Glenfinnan, halfway between Fort William and Mallaig. The local railway viaduct is familiar to all "Harry Potter fans". The "Jacobite Steam Train" runs here, named after the Jacobite Uprising, since "Bonnie Prince Charlie" landed here in 1745 and commenced his claim on the throne[2]. Many know this train better as the

---

[2] The historical background was the "glorious revolution" of 1688: the catholic Stuart-King James II/VII was sent into exile and the protestant King William III of Orange was crowned. The followers of James, mostly stemming out of the Scottish highlands were named Jacobites – after the Latin version of James. Whose grandson Charles Edward Stuart, named "Bonnie Prince Charlie", tried to retake the throne. Initially favored with great success, the endeavor ended in a massive disaster with the decisive defeat at the battle of Culloden April 16th, 1746. Following this, everything that we today consider "typically Scottish" was forbidden: The wearing of kilts, playing of bagpipes and even the Gaelic language.

"Hogwarts-Express". In the episode "The Chamber of Secrets" is the scene with the breathtaking chase in which Harry and Ron try to catch up with the train.

**Glenfinnan on Loch Shiel**

Once we arrive, I have to announce the for me extremely unpleasant news: Unfortunately we have to go back to Fort William and then via road and bridge to the Isle of Skye! As a precaution, I take cover near the door to save myself from any flying objects. Well, they did not drown me in Loch Shiel after all, but thinking to myself, instead absorbed the message with astonishingly calmness: "Why are you hiding from us? Did you think we would beat you to death?" Well, we are in Scotland... I am getting more and more of an inkling that we have become a really well established community!

In the meantime, the guests have suggested that the unpleasantly free space in the back row should be occupied half-days by volunteers.

Now I am starting to really love my guests. Landing on the Isle of Skye, the rain beating from all sides, our short stop becomes more a fight for survival against the rain god! My "fighters", prepared for anything and superbly equipped with wetsuit, leave on the hunt for original photo motifs. They steadfastly accept the challenge of this horizontal precipitation and bravely weather the wind-swept deluge! This is how I love them, my guests. Just don't let it get you down, "Braveheart" sends his regards, Scotland is after all not for "wimps". A picture of the picturesque stone bridge with heavy rain from the front is certainly a snapshot with great value, since certainly not everyone possesses such a rarity.

As we continue to our hotel in Gairloch, our bus increasingly transforms into a steam bath. Our driver gives his best driving on the sometimes single-road track and we arrive at our hotel in a good mood. Check-in in the rain is certainly not great, but that evening everyone can enjoy the wonderful beach in front of the hotel rain free.

In most hotels, a king-size bed is provided for couples (that is a continuous mattress and one duvet!), which does not especially arouse enthusiasm amongst couples who can look back on many years together. Therefore, in most cases, I am more likely to hear from my couples the wish for two separate beds. Sometimes the opposite does happen though. Before dinner, a gentleman complained to me that he and his partner had to sleep again in two separate beds, which are not pushed together easily. They really could not explore their affections fully. To be honest, he described his issue much more drastically. Of course, this is an urgent problem that a tour guide has to solve ... And the missing suitcase still has not turned up either. Up until then, I had already made several phone calls to the British Airways hotline and we are slowly losing hope. How great is it then that our daily stops provide at least one "gift shop" at the sights. The concerned party returns daily with new T-shirts to the bus.

Is British Airways now trying to support the Scottish tourism through a delay tactic? As a belated generous gesture to compensate for centuries of brutal draining and squeezing of Scotland by England? Well, probably not. Despite everything, we spend a wonderful evening in Gairloch and start the next morning towards Inverness. The "Capital of the Highlands" is certainly not one of the most beautiful cities in the country, but is a must-visit for everyone traveling in this region.

On the last day of our trip, we first stop in Pitlochry in the morning, where we will visit a whiskey distillery over lunch. After our arrival, I first take a walk with all those inquisitive to the dam and local fish ladder. This is a round trip of just under an hour back to the town center. Since the distillery is on the outskirts, we take the bus there with the plan that we will return to the bus parking lot in the center to have a stopover in beautiful Pitlochry. In the afternoon, with another stop at the Firth of Forth bridges, I plan to get to our hotel in Livingston, where I will say goodbye. From there, I planned to take the train to Glasgow, where I booked a hotel, to fly back to Germany the following day. Now a tour of a distillery with the associated sample in the form of a "wee dram" - a small sip (which is usually truly very small - in that respect the Scots fulfill the prejudice of being stingy!) does not seem to agree with everyone. On the way to the parking lot in the center of town, a drive of about five minutes, I announce the departure time for the afternoon. I repeat those important organizational times over and over! Nevertheless, a guest approaches me in the parking lot with the question: "And when are we leaving again?" Slightly aggrieved, I state that the time had been announced several times. But this guest is absolutely convinced that he has not received any such information. So of course, I share the time with him again! Since we are close to the end of the trip, I no longer desire to create two free places. Rather, I am gripped by the ambition to bring the tour to a happy close, complete and with satisfied guests. Despite all the adversities and mishaps, a very nice end of the trip is already within our sight!

But after the break, this thought reveals itself to be a fallacy! We want to leave at 3 p.m.; ten minutes prior, almost all of the guests are at the bus, with the exception of a young single traveler. I asked the group if anyone knew where she could be. The answer: "Yes, she wants to redo the round from the morning and set off shortly before 3 p.m." causes me to almost lose my composure. What? This might still take at least half an hour!

After a few hectic phone calls, she returns to the parking lot slightly distraught and now complete we can commence our last trip to the hotel. However, after a few minutes, this trip will come to a several hours long standstill.

On the A9 in the direction of Perth, we drive just as far until the road becomes a two-lane road and from there it jams! The cars turn around; police cars drive past us. The bus driver and I look at each other in disbelief and probably both think: "That cannot be true! The traffic jam will probably dissolve soon", since it is well known that hope always dies last. But it doesn't dissolve. A serious accident occurred shortly before the village of Dunkeld, the road is completely closed; there are no alternative routes for us with this bus. So, we are forced to line up and make the best of the situation. A very nice group photo is taken, addresses are exchanged, everything left to eat and the last cigarettes are thrown into the mix. We are already an unfortunately tried and tested group and so we only perceive this situation as the culmination of our unrest, bad luck and breakdown trip! In total, our involuntary stay on this road ends up lasting ca. 5 hours. Exhausted but relieved, we arrive at our hotel at around 10 p.m. There is even still something to eat for us and everyone will surely remember this trip as unforgettable - at least it is for me, which I am proving here!

**Eilean Donan Castle**

**Piper in the Glen Coe**

# 6. "Lady Annag MacZoch"

Let's go to Scotland again and I am really looking forward to it! It is the beginning of September 2018. I meet my tour group with the bus driver Georg at our agreed upon meeting place just before the border to the Netherlands.

The comfortable night ferry from Amsterdam / Ijmuiden takes us to Newcastle in Northern England. The next morning, we make our way through the beautiful English National Park Northumberland and the border region Borders. Passing the Scottish capital of Edinburgh, we continue over the Firth of Forth to Pitlochry, our accommodation for this trip in the heart of Scotland.

From here, we make many beautiful excursions, including one to the legendary Loch Ness and to Inverness. This city calls itself somewhat cockily "the Capital of the Highlands". And it is here, after some gentle encouragement from our driver Georg, that I decide to become a Scottish Lady!

Even during previous trips, I have always told my guests that anyone who wants to buy property in Scotland has the opportunity to become Lady or Lord / Laird (this is the Scottish version of the

Lord), since the title is bound to a plot of land. So now, there are quite a number of business-minded land and title vendors.

Up until this trip, I had not considered such a purchase for myself, but now I am on the hunt with Georg. He's got it into his head to become Lord George and I am infected by his enthusiasm!

Also, with every purchase of a parcel of land, no matter how small, the buyer protects this plot from unwanted interference and thus contributes as well to the preservation of Scotland's inherent landscape. So ultimately, it is a form of landscape protection and the preservation of wilderness in Scotland. For example, the owner can thus contribute to the wildcat population's and other wild animal's protection.

"So it's also a good contribution for environmental protection!" I think to myself. After the city of Inverness tour with my guests, I set out to buy two "plots of land" and thus the titles for both of us.

In a souvenir shop in the pedestrian zone, run by a German emigrant, I find it. Here I get all necessary documents with an access number to be used to log in and register on the relevant homepage.

This is also possible with a fantasy name. I choose "Lady Annag", the Gaelic nickname of Anna and the surname MacZoch.

As a new landowner, I will then receive my personal certificate by mail. For a little over 30 pounds, I am buying a plot of around 30x30 centimeters, one "square foot", and can therefore now introduce myself as Lady Annag MacZoch!

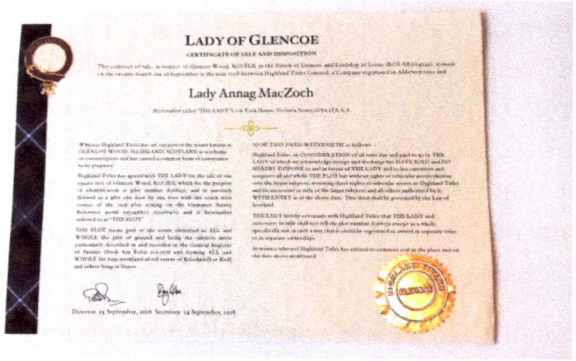

The prefix "Mac" comes from Gaelic, the original language of the Scots, and has the meaning: "Son of". The surname "MacGregor" can be translated as "son of Gregor". For women there was once the corresponding prefix "Nic" meaning "daughter of". The naming has changed over time though; women now also use the prefix "Mac" for their family name. That is why I chose the fantasy name "MacZoch" for myself and had it registered.

Anyone can become Lady or Lord with their desired name: https://www.highlandtitles.de/

### *More on Pitlochry and the Braemar Highland Games…*

*Pitlochry is about a 30-minute drive north of Perth on the A9, which is an important thoroughfare from Perth to Inverness and thus right through the country. It is said about Pitlochry that this small town of around 2800 people lies in the heart of Scotland. Its central location and the lovely center, which has already been crowned "Winner in Bloom" several times for its public flower displays, make this attractive and cozy place an ideal location for excursions into the surrounding areas. Some of the local attractions are two whiskey distilleries, the Edradour & Blair Athol, the fish ladder at Loch Faskally with its new visitor center, and the festival building, once inaugurated by Prince Charles in the 190th.*

*A highlight for all guests in Scotland in September is definitely the visit to the famous "Highland Games" of Braemar, which always take place on the first Saturday of the month. These are mainly sports competitions in sometimes quite unusual disciplines. But also "see and be seen", collecting for charitable causes, and, ultimately, lots of fun and having a good time define the atmosphere in the small and tranquil town in the Cairngorm Mountains. With around 900 inhabitants, in the travel high season however, this cozy place is rather geared towards tourists from the hiking and outdoor variety. The omnipresent musical backdrop on those days is predominantly defined by bagpipes, which provides the "typically Scottish" flair. The many festival-goers in their kilts and sometimes quite exotic outfits with wild animal skins slung over their shoulders, as well as the ladies in rubber boots and hats à la Ascot are certainly a delectable feast for the eyes and that not only for non-Scots.*

*Braemar is the venue for the most famous "Highland Games" in Scotland! Guests from all over the world and many visitors from the surrounding area want to be present when the athletes face the somewhat idiosyncratic and sometimes quite unusual disciplines.*

*These games probably go all the way back to the 11th century and were once used to determine the fastest and strongest fighters for the king. The Braemar Games have been ennobled by Queen Victoria's visit in the mid-19th century. She loved staying at Balmoral Castle, ca. 15 kilometers away. Since then it has been a tradition that the Queen spends her vacation in this castle at the beginning of September and attends the games in Braemar.*

*Around 3 p.m. the time has arrived. The barriers on the streets have been set up and the many visitors are hoping for a particularly good photo!*

*The arrival of the Queen with her entourage is duly celebrated each year. The march to greet her with the seemingly innumerable "Drums & Pipe" bands (drums and bagpipes) is overwhelming and guarantees visitors goose bumps! The noise level alone is impressive. Followed by the British national anthem and the Queen and her companion then take their place of honor in the lavishly decorated royal pavilion.*

*With a lot of fun and humor, the best in each disciplines are determined and celebrated: Among other things, races over various distances, tugs of war, stone throwing, hammer throwing, as well as dances with a particularly complicated sequence of steps can be witnessed. The unmistakable sound of bagpipes is omnipresent!*

**The royal limousine is coming!**

*The afternoon highlights are "Tossing the Caber", the throwing of tree trunks, as well as the visit of the Queen! This special sports discipline probably originated in a time before our modern infrastructure of freeways and roads, when soldiers had to improvise the building of bridges in impassable terrain. Then trees had to be felled and the trunks thrown over the rivers: the closer they landed to each other, the better the guarantee, that the soldiers could cross once done. Today the aim of the competitors is to throw the tree trunks, weighing about 50 to 60 kilograms, in such a manner that they rotate fully 180 degrees and then ideally land in an exactly straight line: In earlier times, this would have given them a perfect bridge.*

*Today it is more about entertainment for all. The respective competitions are completed in a very serious and sportsman-like manner, but fun and entertainment are in the forefront of the event. The visitors are always thrilled when the children's "sack race" starts. This event also takes place in the presence of the Queen, who obviously enjoys it immensely. It is also her duty to present the winners of the respective disciplines with their awards. Afterwards the Queen is of course duly bidden farewell: A large number of musicians (again drums & pipes, of course) accompany the limousines of the royal visitors on their departure, accompanied also by huge applause and standing ovations!*

*The whole town is the unique setting on this day and part of this extraordinary event, which takes place in an amazingly relaxed atmosphere. Along the roads into town, families and their friends gather for a picnic in the private gardens, which provide an exclusive view of the colorful events.*

*Many charity stands line the street where people collect, for example for guide dogs; the Rotary Club also has a stand in the center of town. Here, everyone can roll the dice for just a small bet and has the chance to win a gigantic bottle of whiskey!*

*At the corner, in front of the war memorial on the bridge, you can find a rustic guitar player, like every year. He is a true original who cannot be missing on this day.*

*It is the overall flair, which turns this small, cozy place into a unique stage for a day. And the special atmosphere is shaped by the variety: It is the wonderful mixture of the royal visit in the afternoon, the extremely committed and friendly residents, and the many guests from all around the world! The mix of local color and international flair creates the special ambiance! And all of this, happens in a very relaxed and laid back manner, with no special safety precautions or noticeable restrictions for the visitors.*

*These games, also known as the "Oatmeal Olympics", can now be found all over the country and also abroad: But for me, the Braemar games will always be the one and true "Highland Games"!*

**The legendary tree trunk throwing:
Tossing the Caber!**

# 7. "Agent 0076 on a Secret Mission"

I am Lady Annag, Her Majesty's secret undercover
agent with the code number 0076. I will soon be
taking on missions in Ireland and southern
England, but I do not like to "jump in at the deep
end"! Before starting my assignments, I always
want to get the lay of the land, and preferably to
do so in person. So, how do I best proceed?

A have a great idea! For my professional development with a view to future assignments, I book an organized group trip to Ireland and the south of England. I register incognito as a normal guest. "It couldn't be any better," I think to myself. "I can only benefit from this and I will learn a lot. All in all, it should definitely be an extremely interesting experience." Towards the other guest but more so towards the tour guide, I will behave like a completely normal traveler. "Undercover" on the way to unknown destinations on an organized group trip. How exciting.

Our tour guide greets us at Dublin Airport. I am curious about the other guest and I am really looking forward to this trip! Now I lean back in the bus, relax, and give myself over to whatever will come. In the next few days, I will certainly have many new and valuable experiences as a guest of a tour group. After arriving at our hotel on the outskirts of Dublin, no further group activities are planned that afternoon. So I set out inconspicuously to explore the vicinity of our hotel (at least that is what I thought, but I meet some of my fellow travelers during my exploration) and buy some snacks for the next few days.

As on the following days, on the eve of our arrival, we sit down for dinner without our tour guide. This is not a problem for me, as I know the local customs very well from my previous assignments. But my fellow travelers are somewhat confused and therefore our first meal together is delayed. Since I am now hungry after the long day, I explain to my fellow travelers that drinks such as beer and wine always have to be fetched at the bar in advance to dinner and that no food can be ordered unless all of the guests are seated at the tables.

The next day, we went on a city tour followed by a walk through Dublin; the afternoon is at our leisure. At the end of the official program, our tour guide invites me for coffee. It is with a slight apprehension that I accept this invitation. I however do not want to expose my secret mission and hope rather to extract, through roundabout questioning, some worthy information about Ireland. To my regret, the "technical information" about Ireland, which I am aiming for, comes to a rather quick end. He deflects my questions by replying "I have no clue, but these a really interesting. I'll have to research this for the future." This is a real shame, and I realize that I will not get any further specialized information this way and decide to leave it at this one attempt. The next day, our tour of Ireland starts now for real; after breakfast, we drive across the country to Galway on the west coast. The weather is typically Irish, very fluctuating. That day, I discover a new "hobby". I keep a tally of the many rainbows that we get to see on our trip: seven on this day alone! Unfortunately, we also learn on this drive that our afternoon boat trip to the Cliffs of Moher has been cancelled due to strong wind. As a substitute, a stop at the visitor center for all guests has been added. I am happy with the spontaneous program change and enjoy the fantastic view.

**The secret agent Lady Annag 0076 incognito at the Cliffs of Moher**

The sea is very rough today; the spray reaches me even at a height of ca. 120 meters. The view at this superb point in the west of Ireland is breathtaking! The early arrival at the hotel at around 5 p.m., and the about 45 minutes' walk to the center of Ennis, compels me and some of my fellow travelers to rather explore the hotel bar prior to dinner and sample the local drinks[3]. It

---

[3] We struggle choosing from the lavish number of Irish **whiskeys** on offer, which differ from the Scottish whisky in the spelling with an "e" and its triple distillation. This makes them just a bit smoother. Probably the most know ones are Jameson, Tullamore Dew and Bushmills from Northern Ireland. The best-known Irish beer is most likely the "Guinness", a top-fermented black beer with a cream-colored head, which is known as "stout". Definitely just as good, but a little less famous, is "Murphy's" from Cork. My favorite first drink is usually a "cider", a refreshingly fruity beer made from apples. The well-known Irish brands are "Magners" and "Bulmers". A decision in favor of one of the many top-fermented "ales" is very difficult: there are, for example, the well-known "Kilkenny" and "Smithwick's". These days, the bottom-fermented and low to medium hopped lager is the most consumed beer in Ireland: Heineken Ireland has the largest share of sales in Ireland. Other well-known Irish lagers are Harp Lager (produced by Guinness Brewery) and Carling LagerKinsale Irish Lager.

ends up being a very funny and entertaining evening in the hotel pub. The next day, our journey takes us through Killarney National Park to Muckross House and here we spend an eventful day. On a carriage ride through the beautiful park, I unexpectedly get to prove myself as our coach driver's assistant and at the end of the tour; I discover that our draft horse always receives a Guinness after the work is done.

I am impressed and touched as well by this particular curiosity of Irish patriotism. How strange and exceedingly lovely: a carriage horse enjoying a typical Irish after-hour beer! I am giving it an apple.

We spend our next night in Waterford on the southern coast. The origins of this city, as well as those of Dublin, Limerick, Cork and Wexford, go back to the time of the Vikings[4].

---

[4] The Viking Age spanned a period of around 300 years, starting with the raid of the Lindisfarne monastery, off the northeastern coast of England in 793. Following the time of plunder, settlements and trade centers were established. Normandy in northern France is named after the "Northmen". Multiple sieges of Paris finally prompted the French king to agree to a Viking settlement at the mouth of the Seine. The end of the

The phone rings at 5 a.m., a wake-up call received by all guests to remind them of our early departure. After a very early and rather subdued breakfast, we drive to the ferry, which will take us from Ireland to Wales. At dawn, we say goodbye to our friendly Irish driver with a well-filled envelope and warm words of thanks.

At the ferry terminal, we learn that a suitcase trolley will shortly be arriving for our luggage and that we will then take the bus onto the ferry - unfortunately we are not informed of the exact time of departure. For me as secret undercover agent this is again a very exciting moment, to get to know the organizational process here at the ferry terminal for future missions. Our tour guide

---

Viking Age is listed as the year 1066: William the Conqueror was a descendant of the first settled Northmen in today's Normandy and was intended to be the successor of the English king. However, there were other aspiring to sit on the English throne. Wilhelm then awaited the outcome of the Battle of Stamford Bridge near York in Central England: Harold Godwinson defeated Harald Hadradar from Norway. Afterwards, the winner had to send his weakened and exhausted troops in a hurry to Hastings on the southern coast where he then was defeated by Wilhelm.

enters the terminal building with the words that we might want to use the toilets here. The baggage trolley arrives very soon and we check in our suitcases, then everyone gradually strolls into the terminal building. Our tour guide has not returned by then, so we take care of his suitcase as well. However, his document bag, the guests prefer to take with them into the terminal in order to hand it over personally. When I make my way inside shortly afterwards, I encounter him and I ask if there is still time for coffee. His answer is quite rude. Did he sleep badly? As I learn afterwards, he is not happy about someone delivering his briefcase to him. As a thank you, this helpful guest is very rudely reprimanded. We just wanted to do him a favor! During the three-hour ferry crossing to reach Wales, he is not to seen again.

Shortly before our arrival at our destination in the Welsh Fishguard, we meet on the car deck indicated as our meeting point. Standing in exhaust fumes, we wait with the tour guide. He does not react to our questions and rather signals with his posture: "Do not talk to me!" We are now a little irritated ... After a long while, he questions a ferry employee and we are directed back up the stairs, which, however, soon stalls. After a few minutes, another guest asks: "What are we doing here? Why the stall?" Our tour guide reacts with a weak shrug. His sympathy levels now reach a low point. "You don't need to collect anything for him," one of my fellow travelers whispers to me. At some point we reach daylight, take a bus from the ferry to the terminal building where we receive our luggage. However, one suitcase is missing! "Firstly, everyone to the bus, maybe it is there", is the announcement. But only much later is it found in the terminal. With lots of time lost, we finally cast off. This will shorten our stay in Cardiff, we learned at the start of the journey. At 5 p.m. we arrive at the hotel, which is located near Newport on the M4, our dinner is at 7 p.m. and so the hotel bar again makes a killing.

The next morning we all make it to the bus at the agreed upon time to load the luggage so we can leave on time: However, our tour guide is missing! After a few minutes of waiting, I ask our driver if he has his phone number. In doing so, in this moment, I am already jeopardizing my secrecy as an undercover agent and I am also getting involved in in something that basically has nothing to do with me, but our day's program is in danger. I want to save this purely selfishly as well as a guest and as a secret undercover agent! "No, I haven't" is the answer of our driver. Spontaneously, I then go to the hotel reception and have them call our tour guide: After it rings several times, I get the message that he overslept and will arrive in 10 minutes. Ok, that can happen to anyone, but after his performance the day before, it really is not very beneficial for him.

In the afternoon, we visit Castle Cothele; the entrance fee was part of an excursion package and not all guests have booked this in advance. Additionally, three of the fellow travelers would like to join our tour and our guide brings them suspiciously quickly through the entrance booth. I cannot help myself and ask more precisely: And as it happens, they did not pay any admission! On our tour through the castle, we then get the following abstruse information in the bedchambers: "Couples had separate bedrooms because the women snored!" Am I hearing correctly? Are you really serious? Is it not usually the other way around? Those are my thoughts in that moment. Further explanations of this kind have all shake their heads in disbelief. How good that I am traveling incognito! At least that is what I still believe.

Because, that afternoon I let one of my fellow travelers seduce me into a "confession" in private: "What are you actually doing all of the time? You cannot be a normal guest, you constantly writing everything down and are double-checking everything! Are you perhaps a tour tester?" Since my disguise is apparently inadequate, I reveal myself to her as a secret undercover agent and tell her that I am using this trip as professional training and that I note down ideas for my future assignments.

We spend the next two nights in Plymouth on the southern English coast. The next morning, we encounter a strange situation on the ferry crossing the River Tamar, which forms the border to Cornwall. Shortly before reaching the ferry terminal, we received the organizational information that we can get off the bus here on the ferry and use the toilets. After this announcement, almost all fellow travelers get up and wait patiently in the center aisle of the bus. However, I am sitting in the far back of the bus and think to myself: "This is not worth it for me. When I finally get off, I can immediately get back on; this journey will only take about 10 minutes." After about 5 minutes, one of the guests asks slightly furious:" When can we get off?" "We cannot get the door open", comes the succinct information from our tour guide. "Well then, thank you very much for this delayed information!", is the slightly irritated reply from the guest. "What was that now?", most everyone is probably wondering at that moment. For me this is another example on the subject of poor communication; I really pity my fellow travelers at this moment! What is made very clear to me here, is the importance of good and clear communication and information sharing in such a situation, I would definitely do this differently...

I am thrilled about the lunchtime stop at "Lands End", which we owe to our bus driver. This is the furthest point in the southwest of the British Isles; the northeastern counterpart is "John o'Groats" in Scotland. The connection of those two places is the greatest possible road distance on the island of good 1406 kilometers, which corresponds roughly to the distance from Hamburg to Monaco. With this tourism infrastructure, "Lands End" is certainly extremely crowded during high season. A visit to the idyllic St. Ives, a true "Pilcher's backdrop", rounds off our stay in Cornwall in the afternoon.

This trip is a very valuable experience for me: As a guest on an organized group trip, I have now experienced all facets of such a journey. With my many insights and the countless ideas for a previously unknown-to-me area, I am already looking forward to my future assignments in Ireland and southern England! In any case, I have received a lot of inspiration of how I am planning my trips to these destinations in the future...

**Not so incognito anymore at Land's End in Cornwall**

## 8. "With a Troll in Lapland"

Anyone who thinks that trolls only exist in Norway or Iceland got it wrong. People in Sweden also believe in these fascinating creatures! Anyone who travels through this magical landscape using their imagination encounters many such trolls!

I am convinced that I have met some of them already several times in Sweden and I am sure that there have been many trolls in some of my tour groups! I am sure that not so long ago, I travelled with a troll in Lapland ... What convinced me, I will recount now in this personal story:

"Once upon a time, there was a cheerful group of travelers who journeyed to the far north of Europe to explore the icy and almost deserted Lapland in Sweden. The brave leader of this group had set off in a German train the day prior and, surprisingly, even arrived at her destination on time! Very early the next morning, the brave yet a bit sleepy heroes met at the designated meeting point, to make their way as group to the airport.

The leader soon noticed that there was obviously a troll in her group of travelers and thought to herself: "Hopefully is this going to work. But maybe it's not that bad ... I'll help him a little and then everything will be ok." So, the brave leader supported the troll through the first trial at airport security and found that he was not wearing any socks! "Oh dear", she thought, "Hopefully it will be not as cold as usually in Lapland; otherwise the troll might freeze off his toes! Certainly there must still be socks in the luggage for the really cold days, and then everything will be all right".

In high spirits and full of anticipation arriving in Lapland, all the daring heroes climbed into the mighty coach, which took them through a snowy winter's wonderland to the Arctic Circle. Here everyone exited and said hello to the polar region, which they wanted to explore thoroughly over the next few days. Only few additional kilometers, separated the courageous warriors from the small town of Jokkmokk, and their cozy accommodation. Now they were finally able to move into their warm and safe private quarters for the coming days and restore their energies.

After a restful night, the band of travelers started, rested and full of anticipation, on a very long journey that was to take them even further into the icy north, all the way to the northernmost city of the country. First, they went to Kiruna and then to a fascinating building made of ice and snow, the famous "Icehotel". The brave heroes wanted certainly also to collect evidence of their special adventures. Therefore, the warriors made a first stop at a lookout point to take many photos in this beautiful landscape. Our troll found it exceedingly difficult to get out of the carriage and then he told the brave leader that he had not even been able to travel until recently. This adventure would be a difficult test for him! He wanted to find out during this trip, whether such a journey was even still possible for him. Although his child advised him against this venture ardently, this troll was very courageous and extremely confident that everything would be well. And besides, a helpful companion had already lent him "walking aids" for his shoes, so now nothing could go wrong. "Where now did the brave leader get her shoes? Are they good and to be bought affordably here in Lapland?" was the question from the troll during this break. Well, the fearless leader had bought her shoes at home. She thought to herself that the troll would have done better to choose a different destination for such a test. It became more and more clear to the lionhearted leader that this troll had not even prepared for the destination Lapland beforehand.[5]

The next day, the group of travelers spent most of their time in the cozy Jokkmokk and enjoyed a wonderful snow-covered winter landscape. At lunchtime, the courageous brave-hearts drove to the reindeer farm. All adventurers were looking forward to meeting the reindeer herders Helena and Rickard Länta. In order to be able to see and feed the animals, the group had wade to the game reserve and needed to deal at times with deep snow. Our committed and extremely helpful

---

[5] Hardly any traveler suspects that in Sweden the smaller towns and cities only provide basic health care in health centers, while in Lapland in particular you have to travel long distances to the nearest hospital. From our hotel in Jokkmokk it is almost 100 kilometers to the next hospital! It has also happened that guests were very surprised by the early onset of dusk (depending on the travel date, this varies a lot: in December it starts to get dark at around 1:30 p.m.) and the freezing temperatures, which at first glance do not seem too cold due to the dry cold. After a few minutes however, these will get painfully noticeable! And with inadequate clothing can actually lead to unpleasant frostbite.

coachman used one of the modern motor scooters to transport our troll. Without his commitment, it would have been impossible for this troll on these rough terrains. He of course did not follow the good advice: "Please watch your steps and stay in the track!", since trolls can be very stubborn and so he promptly ventured into deep snow! The "rescue" only succeeded with combined forces; a troll can be quite heavy. But the ride on the motorized "chained four-wheeler" was visibly a great pleasure for him. His demeanor reminded me slightly of that of the Queen of Great Britain. The troll of course did not even noticed that our coachman had to juggle heavily during this ride. What luck, that our coachman turned out to be a true hero on the "chained four-wheeler"!

The dog sledding the next day was definitely the biggest highlight of this venture for all these traveling daredevils. Some, however, were tested putting on the necessary protective equipment with overalls and suitable snow shoes against the cold. Of course, the bold leader helped her gang with dressing. This time as well, there was another trial to be mastered: The troll was barefoot again! Even some of the others were very surprised. "My medicine man is always happy to see me," was the troll's terse remark. In the afternoon, the intrepid warriors went on a hike along spectacular rapids. Almost all of the daring set out with the bravest of leaders on this adventure, a partly iced over path, they demonstrated their bravery and determination by overcoming all dangers and adversities. However, this path was certainly not suitable for everyone. Some heroes preferred to overcome this difficult hurdle safely stowed in the mighty coach. General relief then marked the joyful reunion at the viewpoint; everyone had mastered this challenge very well and survived it unscathed.

The next day, promised two particularly nice items in Jokkmokk. Without the troll, everyone could have mastered this excursion easily without the mighty carriage, but it was very difficult for him to walk. Thus agreed our attentive coachman, to take the warriors comfortably by bus to their intended destinations. In the local pewter factory, the interested tourists received great information about the manufacture of these high-quality products. The tour through the production facilities ended in the shop with another particularly impressive demonstration of traditional artisanship. The troll could not wait for the tour to end and already started buying his souvenir during the last presentation. His difficulties in paying his due with his a modern plastic card resulted in a rather annoying disturbance...

The next stop on this trip was a wonderful museum. Here the troll exited without his warming cloak. All heroes were offered a transfer back to their quarter with the mighty coach, but only 2.5 hours later! When several other adventurers asked the troll whether it was not appropriate to take his warming cloak with him, the troll only shrugged. After an introduction by the brave leader, the warriors were able to explore the extensive and very varied exhibition about the mountains of Lapland and above all else, about the history and culture of the Sami. A while later in the museum's shop, the leader met the amazingly heroic participant of this venture, who had patiently and sacrificially looked after the troll over the past few days. The troll was already sitting on the bench at the museum entrance. The mighty carriage was far from coming! The truly brave leader asked the troll "Have you already flown in the helicopter?" There is a very nice flight simulation to be found in the museum, which superbly shows the visitor the mountainous region of Lapland. The answer from the troll was: "No, but when will she finally arrive?" The troll was impatiently waiting for his helpful companion from this band of travelers. In the evening a discernable dissonance could be noticed between the two; the troll had probably overused the willingness of his helper...

To the great relief of the fearless leader, the troll survived this journey without frostbite or any other damage. The troll had more luck than brains, because the temperatures in Lapland were very mild, around freezing instead of the usual minus degrees of up to -20°C.

This troll was certainly a great trial for everyone involved, but it was mastered by everyone with a lot of bravery and a sense of community!

Many thanks to Mrs. K. for her self-sacrificing support, she definitely had not booked the additional "troll package"

### More about Lapland ...

*In Kiruna, Sweden's northernmost city, you can visit a lovely wooden church, the architecture of* which is inspired by a Sami tent and Norwegian stave churches. Contributors to the design of the church include: Prince Eugen with an altarpiece and Christian Eriksson with the figure of "Georg as a dragon slayer", a relief on the facade and twelve statues on the roof, which symbolize human feelings, including tenderness, love, compassion and despair. The church was completed in 1912 and was once one of the most beautiful churches in Sweden; it was also depicted on a postage stamp.

At the beginning of the 20th century, Kiruna was built very close to one of the largest iron ore mines in the world. The name comes from the North Sami word giron, the name for ptarmigan, which can be seen on the city's coat of arms. In 1948 the *community Jukkasjärvi, to which this area belonged, was renamed Kiruna and raised to the status of town. Currently, the city is threatened to collapse due to mountain damage. In order to be able to mine the iron ore deposits below the city, a relocation master plan was presented in 2014, that envisages a gradual relocation of the city of Kiruna by 2033. The church is to be preserved and rebuilt at a new location.*

*The world-famous ICEHOTEL in Jukkasjärvi is renewed every winter and will melt in the course of the coming spring. The building material comes from the Torneälv river. In March, the almost crystal-clear blocks of ice are harvested and stored in the freezer until the next winter season. Artists from all over the world apply to design the rooms and it is always fascinating to see the amazing ideas that are brought to life. There are several buildings: the ephemeral hotel and the year-round House-365 with an ice bar and luxury suites. A solar system on the roof generates enough electricity for the cooling system, especially in summer when the sun does not set for a period of several weeks: the so-called polar day. There are also small wooden huts for overnight guests, a reception with a lobby to warm yourself and a permanent building with sanitary facilities and breakfast room.*

*The small town of Jokkmokk with around 2800 inhabitants at current is the traditional winter camp for reindeer herders of the region. The first settlement dates back to 1602. King Charles IX ordered the construction of few marketplaces in northern Sweden in order to be able to reach the scattered native indigenous population of the Sami easier for trade, tax collection and proselytizing. Jokkmokk's "Vintermarknad", winter market, was first held in 1605. Since then, every year, it takes place on the first Thursday, Friday and Saturday in February and is the highlight of the year for the residents. There are up to 40,000 visitors at one time. During the winter market, all accommodations in Jokkmokk and the surrounding area are fully booked and that, months in advance: there will be no winter market in 2021!*

*The name of the indigenous population of Northern Europe is Sami and means "swamp people". They call their settlements "Sapmi". According to their own count, there are around 70,000 Sami, of which around 40,000 live in Norway, around 20,000 in Sweden, around 8,000 in Finland and around 2,000 in Russia. The term "Lapp" developed from the old Finnish as a foreign term meaning "border residents" and therefore had a negative connotation from the beginning. Today the term "Lapp" is considered politically incorrect. The oppression and exploitation has dragged on for many centuries. Since the 1980s, a new self-confidence has however emerged, which is reflected in a national flag (since 1988) and the respective Sami parliaments (since 1993 in Kiruna, Sweden). The many current conflicts are with the "settlers", the Swedes who moved there, the new residents and thus the beneficiaries of the area, especially of the existing mineral resources (iron ore, water, forest)!*

*The traditional routes of the reindeer are severely affected by roads, hydropower plants and forestry. Today the Sami live in a balancing act between the demands of the modern age and theirs traditional way of life. There are around 2500 families in Sweden who live exclusively from reindeer herding.*

*Like the elk, reindeer belong to the deer family. But only the reindeer females also have antlers so that they can better defend their feeding grounds in winter. This way, they are able to track down their food of mosses and lichens through layers of snow several meters thick. The increasingly mild winters however, with alternating thaws and freezing temperatures are currently causing major problems for reindeer herders: The ice means that the animals can no longer track down and reach their food!*

*During the migration in spring and autumn several thousand animals come together; once they reach their destination they split up into small packs of 10 to 15 animals, consisting of either females or males. The "reindeer differentiation" takes place in autumn. The reindeer are "sorted" and the owners recognize their animals by their distinctive ear markings. At that time, the animals are selected for slaughter. For the Sami it is very important to use every part of the reindeer as much as possible: the meat, the fur, the antlers - among other things, and their traditional clothing and the handles on the knives are made from those. The reindeer are the proud property of the Sami. As a visitor, never ask a Sami how many reindeer they have, as that would be tantamount to a personal question about personal finances! If an animal has to be slaughtered, everything will be used if at all possible. The Sami have always lived sustainability; they have never been able to afford waste!*

**Helena Länta in traditional work clothes**

# 9. Info about the Countries: Why Visit?

**I did not list the juicy history of the respective countries here, that, I prefer to tell you in person during my travels ☺...**

## Sweden:

I associate Sweden with red wooden houses, endless forests, hundreds of thousands of lakes, moose, grandiose coastal landscapes, very friendly and relaxed residents, a comprehensive social system and, last but not least, the home of Astrid Lindgren and Henning Mankell.

The Swedish national territory includes the eastern part of the Scandinavian Peninsula and the islands of Gotland and Öland. Sweden has been a member of the European Union since 1995 with the Swedish krona as the national currency, but it is not a member of NATO and has no militarily allegiance. The capital and at the same time the largest city of the country is Stockholm with around 976,000 inhabitants; a good fifth of the approximately 10 million Swedes live in the greater area. The second largest city is Gothenburg with approx. 580,000, in third place is Malmö with approx. 317,000 inhabitants; the south of the country is the most densely populated.

Sweden borders the states of Norway and Finland as well as the Baltic Sea and the easternmost part of the North Sea. The Oresund Bridge opened in 2000 and is a direct land connection to Denmark. Sweden has around 221,800 islands; Gotland (2994 km²), Öland (1347 km², both in the Baltic Sea), and Orust (346 km², north of Gothenburg) are the three largest. The longest extension of the country from north to south is 1572 km, from east to west 499 km. The longest rivers are the Torneälven (522 km), the Dalälven (520 km), and the Klarälven (460 km); the largest lakes are the Vänern (5650 km²), the Vättern (1900 km²), and the Mälaren (1140 km²).

During the last ice age, today's Swedish landscape with the numerous lakes, rivers, and waterfalls was created. The so-called Fennoscandian land elevation began after the ice masses, which had depressed the earth's crust, melted; this has led to a lifting of the land mass of 800 m since the last ice age (around 10,000 BC). Nowadays, the land elevation reaches up to 10-11 mm annually on the Höga Kusten in northern Sweden, in the Stockholm area it is about 6 mm annually. Large parts of the country are flat to hilly; along the Norwegian border, the mountain ranges reach a height of over 2000 m. The highest mountain in Sweden is the Kebnekaise with about 2100 m. The many archipelagos (Schären) were created by the lifting of the land. Nobody knows exactly how many there really are...

In the first half of the 19th century, Sweden was a pronounced agricultural state, in which 90% of the population lived from agriculture. It was not until the second half of the 19th century that extensive industrialization began, which, until the Great Depression of 1929, laid the foundations for the modern industrial society.

Industrialization was initially based on good access to raw materials and on-site processing: For example, iron ore with the smelters in central and northern Sweden, as well as a large number of sawmills along the northeast coast. It was not until the 1890s that a progressive workshop industry emerged, especially in central Sweden: For example, Nobel AB, ASEA (now ABB), LM Ericsson, Alfa Laval, SKF. After the Second World War, Sweden became one of the leading industrial nations in the world: IKEA and SAAB, VOLVO and SCANIA should be mentioned here.

Even the culture and entertainment industry is defined by Swedish names: ABBA, Europe, Roxette had great international successes; Selma Lagerlöf (the first woman to receive the Nobel Prize for Literature), Astrid Lindgren, Henning Wallander, Håkan Nesser, Stieg Larsson and Jonas Jonasson are just a few internationally known and successful authors. August Strindberg, Ingmar Bergman and Greta Garbo are well-known figures in the theater and film industry.

The economic development peaked in the mid-1960s; the number of employees in industry has been falling since the 1970s, and the service sector has increased since then.

Between 1890 and 1930, the foundations for the Swedish social system were laid. After the Social Democratic Labor Party came into power in 1932, the welfare state was established as a political project, known as the "Swedish model" since the 1970s. The Swedish social system covers everyone: from toddlers to municipal childcare to pensioners and municipal elderly care. The last decade in the 20th century brought radical changes.

The economic crisis at the beginning of the 1990s led to cuts in social benefits, and the demographic developments led to a radical restructuring of the pension system, which is now linked to the economic development.

The Kingdom of Sweden is a parliamentary monarchy, since 1973 is King Carl XVI Gustaf its head of state. His tasks are purely representative and ceremonial; he has no political authority and does not take part in political life whatsoever. His successor will eventually be the very popular Crown Princess Victoria.

And finally, a short note about the most famous inhabitant of the Swedish forests. Many visitors to Sweden hope to meet the kings of the wild, but you have to be lucky, and a meeting with a moose in the wild is usually only likely at dusk or early dawn. A visitor can only have a guaranteed moose encounter in one of the many moose parks. And the truth about the red wooden houses, I'll only tell you in Sweden! ☺

**Lapland:**
Ideally, my arrival in Lapland each winter is rewarded with a first look out of the airplane

window onto a winter's wonderland. After a three-hour flight from Germany, I can now breathe in the icy and, above all, clean air. For me, the stillness and vastness of the landscape as well as the friendliness of the people are the special charms of Lapland.

A precise territorial definition of Lapland is very difficult. On the one hand, there are the historical provinces / regions in Sweden and Finland. Also the "Sapmi" settlement region of the indigenous population, of the Sami, can also be equated with Lapland. This region extends from Norway, Sweden and Finland to the Kola Peninsula in Russia, and also includes areas south of the Arctic Circle.

Sami is the name of the indigenous population; the term "Lapp" is now considered politically incorrect.

It is a foreign name and means "border residents", which means that the term has a rather negative connotation. The Sami never had their own state; the life of the reindeer herders was and still is mainly shaped by the seasonal migrations of the reindeer.

Since the rise in awareness in the 1980s, the Sami flag can been seen more and more frequently, but the Sami are a minority; they make only around 4% of the population.

In the field of music, there are now some successful singers who draw attention to the concerns of the Sami, such as Marie Boine from Norway, as well as Sofia Jannok, Maxida Märak, and Jon Hendrik Fjällgren from Sweden. Environmental protection is a big issue. The economic exploitation of resources through forestry, but also with water energy and, above all, mineral resource mining bring serious upheaval in nature and thus also into the reindeer migrations. Forestry is of great economic importance in Sweden and Finland in particular, but so is traditional reindeer herding by the Sami. However, the focus is on mineral resource mining such as iron ore in Sweden (in Gällivare and especially in Kiruna with one of the largest mines in the world), copper in Norway, and nickel and apatite in Russia.

„Sameting" is the Nordic name for the parliamentary representations of the Sami in Finland (since 1973), Sweden (since 1993) and Norway (since 1989). These institutions have the task of implementing the cultural self-determination of this minority. The name is based on the old Germanic Thing assemblies. An alternative, internationally used designation is "Sami Parliament". The Kola Sámi Assembly is an elected assembly that was founded in 2010 by the Sami people of the Kola Peninsula in Russia, modeled on the Sámi parliaments in the Nordic countries, but is not recognized by the Russian government.

Lapland is extremely sparsely populated: There are around 2 inhabitants per km², the majority live in the cities on the coast, outside the cities there is almost no population. If you are looking for solitude and silence, you should visit Lapland!

On the Baltic Sea, the taiga landscape is undulating; you find mountain heights of a good 2000 meters in the Fjäll on the Swedish-Norwegian border; on the Kola Peninsula in Russia, the heights reach up to 1200 meters. The largest and longest rivers in Lapland are the Torneälven (Sweden: 410 km), the Piteälven (Sweden: 400 km), the Luleälven (Sweden: 450 km), the Kemijoki (Finland: 550 km) and the Ivalojoki (Finland: 180 km).

The largest cities are Kiruna (Sweden: approx. 17,000), Gällivare (Sweden: 8,500), Tromsø (Norway: approx. 77,000), Narvik (Norway: 21,850), Rovaniemi (Finland: 63,000), Irani (Finland: 6,900) and Murmansk (Russia: 307.257).

The Gulf Stream favors the Norwegian coast: Narvik is ice-free all year round, the Gulf of Bothnia, the northern Baltic Sea, freezes over in winter. The climate varies from cool-temperate on the west coast to cold-temperate and subpolar and can be very extreme. Over the course of the year, temperatures can fluctuate from plus 30°C to significantly less than minus -30°C. More rain falls in the west. The further east you go, the drier and more continental the climate becomes. The current global warming is taking place twice as fast in Lapland as in the southern regions with related drastic changes, especially for reindeer herders. Last winter it was very mild and there were repeated thaws. The subsequent frost led to ice layers so that the reindeer could not find any food: this is a very big problem for the reindeer herders!

The wildlife in Lapland is dominated by reindeer and moose, both of which belong to the deer family. There are also bears, wolves, lynxes and wolverines, a species of marten. These are the natural enemies of the reindeer, as are the eagles. Due to climate change, the arctic fox is facing ever greater competition from the red fox, who immigrated from the south. The so-called boreal forest is defined by spruces and pines. Deciduous trees such as birch, mountain ash, poplar, aspen and willow also grow in suitable locations. Further to the north, mosses and lichens dominate the barren and rather treeless landscape. The orange cloudberry (Hjorton in Swedish and Lakka in Finish) looks like a blackberry, has a bitter taste (similar to the North German sea buckthorn) and is a specialty of Lapland.

## Great Britain:

The United Kingdom of Great Britain and Northern Ireland, or United Kingdom for short, with the international abbreviation UK or GB, is the largest island nation in Europe. The United Kingdom is a union of the four parts of England, Wales, Scotland on the main island and Northern Ireland. The British flag (the "Union Jack" or "Union Flag") is a combination of the flags of England, Scotland and Northern Ireland.

With around 66.4 million inhabitants, the UK / GB is the third most populous country in Europe after Russia and Germany.

It is a founding member of NATO as well as the United Nations; is a nuclear power, a permanent member of the UN Security Council and one of the G7 countries. From 1973 to 2020, Great Britain was a member of the EEC and the European Union. The result of the referendum on June 23, 2016 led to the exit from the European Union, the so-called Brexit. The government, like the royal family, is based in London, the British capital.

Some territories are closely related to the United Kingdom, but are independent from it under international law. This applies to the Isle of Man and the Channel Islands, which are owned by the British Crown and are not part of the "United Kingdom".

The Commonwealth of Nations of today is an association of independent states that can be seen as the successor to the British Empire. The foundation builds the reaction to the efforts of autonomy from its Dominions (Canada, South Africa, Australia and New Zealand) at the beginning of the 20th century, which should thereby tie them to the Empire. In 1926, it was established that the "Dominions" are autonomous communities within the British Empire, with equal rights, in no way subordinate to others, but linked as members of the Commonwealth by loyalty to the Crown. The status of the member states was rewritten in 1931. From a purely constitutional point of view, the only connection between the United Kingdom and the Dominions was allegiance to the Crown. With the accession of India (1947), Ceylon (today Sri Lanka) (1948) and Pakistan (1949), which belonged to British India before their independence, the modern Commonwealth (New Commonwealth) emerged. These changes were recorded in the London Declaration of 1949. In 1952, the previous Dominions were renamed Commonwealth Realms. In 1957, with the former British colony of Gold Coast / Ghana, a Central African country joined the Commonwealth for the first time. Today the Commonwealth of Nations is comprised of 54 member states.

**England:**

With around 130,400 km², England is the largest and most densely populated part of the United Kingdom and lies in the southern section of the island of Great Britain.

London (with almost 9 million inhabitants) is the capital of England and that of the whole of the United Kingdom. England's population of over 55 million people makes up almost 85% of the UK.

In contrast to Scotland, Wales or Northern Ireland, England has neither its own state parliament nor its own state government. These tasks are carried out by the Parliament and the Government of the United Kingdom.

England practices the free market, has an advanced infrastructure and is one of the strongest regions in Europe in terms of inflation, interest rates and unemployment. The official currency of England is the pound sterling. It is held by many states as a currency reserve and is one of the most important currencies in the world after the US dollar and the euro. England makes up most of the UK's economy, largely because London is / was one of the world's largest financial centers. The country is a leader in the chemical and technical industries, particularly in the aerospace, defense and software industries. The Bank of England, founded in 1694, is the central bank of the United Kingdom.

The geography of the country is characterized by low hills and plains, especially in central and southern England. The highest mountain in England is Scafell Pike in the Cumbrian Mountains at 978 meters. The longest and most famous river in the country is the Thames (346 km). England has a rather humid and warm climate due to the Gulf Stream. Compared to countries on the same latitude, England has a warmer climate and varied weather, influenced by both warm subtropical air and cold polar air.


**Northern Ireland:**
Since 1921, Northern Ireland has been part of the United Kingdom and consists of six of the nine counties in the historic Irish province of Ulster in the north of the island. Northern Ireland is more densely populated than the Republic of Ireland and has a higher degree of industrialization.

The Northern Irish coast is about 500 km long. The island of Rathlin in the northeast is part of

Northern Ireland. The border with the Republic of Ireland is almost 500 kilometers long. The percentage of area of the entire Irish island is around 16 percent, while the share in the population lies by just under 30 percent.

There are three mountain ranges: in the northwest the Sperrin Mountains, in the northeast the Antrim Plateau (highest point is the Trostan, 551 m), in the southeast the Morne Mountains (852 m). The largest lake in Northern Ireland and thus also that of the British Isles is Lough Neagh west of Belfast with an area of 392 square kilometers and a maximum depth of 25 m. A natural monument worth seeing is the Giant's Causeway, the "dam of the giant", with around 40,000 basalt columns by the ocean, protected and cared for by the National Trust on the north coast of Antrim.

Northern Ireland is part of the United Kingdom but is not part of Great Britain. In 1972, the Northern Ireland Office (Abbreviation NIO) was created in London, which is led by an Irish minister. The ministry is responsible for the criminal justice system, the police force and the welfare of victims of politically motivated crimes.

Northern Ireland has the Executive office with the First Minister and Deputy First Minister of Northern Ireland as well as ten regional ministries covering agriculture, culture, arts and leisure, education, the environment, finance and human resources, health, economics, employment and training and regional development and social development. With this ministry set-up, the intention is to create a counterbalance in Belfast and thus promote the growing together of the whole of Ireland. The UK subsidizes the Northern Irish government spending with more than £9 billion annually.

The largest Protestant community is the Calvinist Reformed Presbyterian Church with about 19 percent. Scottish in origin, she is called the "Church of Scotland". The "Church of Ireland" is Anglican, but unlike in England, there has been no state church since 1871. About 250,000 people (14% of the population) belong to the Anglican community of the "Church of Ireland", whose archbishop resides in Armagh and who is also responsible for the approximately 70,000 members in the Republic of Ireland. About 41% of Northern Irish call themselves Roman Catholic. The seat of the Primate of All Ireland is also in Armagh. The Catholic Primate and the Irish

Bishops' Conference are institutions of all of Ireland.

**Republic of Ireland (Ireland):**

The Republic of Ireland is comprises of about five sixths of the island and a large number of smaller offshore islands. The capital and largest city of Ireland is Dublin. Around a third of the total of around 5 million inhabitants live in the metropolitan area of Dublin. Ireland borders Northern Ireland in the north, and thus the United Kingdom, and has been a member of the European Union since 1973. The majority of the population professes the Roman Catholic faith.

Long impoverished and therefore affected by emigration, Ireland has now transformed itself into a highly modern, in some areas multicultural industrial and service society. Every year around 10 million foreign tourists visit the country.

In 2018, Ireland was the second richest country in Europe in terms of gross domestic income per capita and the fifth richest in the world. Up until the 1990s, Ireland was an economically underdeveloped country compared to other EU countries. Especially the USA, brought investments to Ireland in search of locations for export into the European regions, which led to much immigration from Eastern Europe. Because of this economic development, Ireland is known as the "Celtic Tiger". However, Ireland was hit particularly hard by the financial crisis of 2007, because the growing prosperity was also based on a real estate bubble that eventually "burst". In addition, the Irish economy is very dependent on foreign direct investments (FDIs). The very lax regulation of the financial sector attracted many foreign banks, but Ireland's economy as a whole is heavily indebted abroad. The total of outstanding loans, derivatives and mortgage loans from Irish banks is nearly four times the gross domestic product. With real estate prices now falling, many Irish households are overly indebted. From the first quarter of 2008, Ireland was in recession for several years; in 2014, Ireland finally emerged from the crisis. The gross domestic product even grew in 2015 by 7.8%. With that, Ireland shows the sixth largest economic growth in the world and the largest economic growth in Europe.

In the interior of the island, are mostly plains that are enclosed by hilly areas. The Shannon River, which runs north to south, is the longest on the island at around 370 km. Lough Corrib is the largest lake in Ireland and after Lough Neagh, which is part of Northern Ireland, the second largest on the Irish island. The highest mountain is the Carrauntoohil with 1039 m (other names Carrantuohill, Carrantual, Carntuohil). It is located in the southwest of the island in the Macgillicuddy's Reeks. There are a number of national parks spread across the country.

Most of the cultural life takes place in the few major centers of Dublin, Cork, Galway and Limerick. Life outside of these cities in the very sparsely populated country side is tranquil and largely characterized by agriculture and fishing. Nevertheless, there is in some areas a growing increase in tourism, especially in the region around the River Shannon. The arts are promoted primarily through the Arts Council, a government appointed body responsible for developing, supporting and promoting of Irish art.

Irish music is best known for its typical instruments such as the fiddle (violin), whose playing is characterized by the wild Irish style, the flute, especially the tin whistle, and the harp, which is the oldest Irish instrument. Although many countries shows a loss of interest in regards to folk music by the younger generation, traditional Irish music continues to be popular with Irish youth. Internationally successful artists and bands are: U2, The Dubliners, The Cranberries, The Corrs, Enya, Chris de Burgh, Bob Geldorf, Van Morrison and many more.

Dancing is one special element of Irish music: tap dance, set dance and formation dance are very popular and have a long tradition.

Ireland has also produced a large number of eminent writers, including Nobel Prize winners William Butler Yeats, George Bernard Shaw, Samuel Beckett and Seamus Heaney. Other well-known Irish writers are Jonathan Swift, Oscar Wilde, James Joyce and Bram Stoker.


**Scotland:**
Finally back in Scotland! I am looking forward to countless sheep on and by the road, to Scottish whisky, to bagpipe music and to Scots in kilts, to the barren coastal landscape, to the heather-covered peaks, to the good, pure air and to haggis, neeps & tatties!

The largely autonomous part of the United Kingdom of Great Britain and Northern Ireland consists of the northern third (approx. 78,000 km²) of the largest European island Great Britain and several archipelagos and has around 5.5 million inhabitants. The capital of Scotland is Edinburgh with around 480,000 inhabitants, but Glasgow is the most populated city with around 600,000 inhabitants. The Kingdom of Scotland and the Kingdom of England were ruled in personal union from 1603; in 1707 the two states were united to form the Kingdom of Great Britain.

In 1999, Scotland regained its own parliament. Since then, the Scottish Parliament with the First Minister (comparable to Prime Minister and State Governors, currently Nicola Sturgeon) and the Scottish Government have been responsible for most aspects of domestic policy. The official seat of these institutions is Edinburgh. However, as part of the United Kingdom, Scotland does not have its own head of state.

Scotland is divided into three geographic regions: the Highlands, the Central Lowlands and the Southern Uplands. The highest mountain in Scotland (and all of Great Britain) is Ben Nevis near Fort William. The rugged landscape of the Highlands is defined by many lakes and the deeply set estuaries, which in Scotland are called Loch, the best known are Loch Ness and Loch Lomond.

To the west is the archipelago of the Inner and Outer Hebrides with the Isle of Skye and Lewis / Harris. To the north of Scotland are the Orkney Islands and the Shetland Islands. The main population lives in the Central Belt between Edinburgh and Glasgow.

The climate is temperate with varying weather. There is a saying that in Scotland you can experience all seasons in one day, another on is: If you don't like the weather, just wait 5 minutes ...

In general, the weather in west of Scotland is warmer than in the east, since the Gulf Stream of the Atlantic has water warmer than the North Sea. In winter, snowfall is only to be expected inland at higher altitudes.

The apostle Andrew is the national saint and patron saint of the country. Every year, on the 30th of November in his honor, St. Andrews Day is celebrated, a national holiday in Scotland. The flag of Scotland (English Saltire) is based on the St. Andrew's cross. Scotland has been a predominantly Protestant country since the introduction of the Reformation in 1560. The Scottish National Church (Church of Scotland, Kirk) follows a strict Calvinist Presbyterian Reformed theology and liturgy introduced by the reformer John Knox. After the introduction of the Reformation, however, the Roman Catholic faith did not completely disappear from Scotland, but rather remained, especially in the remote areas of the Highlands. In the 19th century, the number of Catholics increased significantly because of immigration from neighboring Ireland, and since the EU's eastward enlargement in 2004, numerous migrants from Catholic countries such as Poland and Lithuania have entered the country as well.

The oil production in the North See defines the Scottish economy; the city of Aberdeen is an important center. Since the 1970th, here the oil business has replaced fishing. Scottish whisky exports were around £4.7 billion in 2018. The largest customer was the EU (£1.4 billion); the US imported £1.04 billion worth of Scotch whisky.

The so-called creative sector (literature, film, fashion, software and computer games) contributed to the Scottish economy in 2010 with a turnover of £4.8 billion. In 2011, these industries employed around 64,000 people.

More than three quarters of the area of Scotland is used for agriculture in the form of arable and pasture farming. The main crops are barley, wheat, oats and potatoes, along with vegetables and fruit. In the Highlands, the Islands and the Southern Uplands, sheep breeding dominates, and cattle breeding also plays a major role in general. Around half of the privately owned land is part of large estates dedicated to hunting red deer and grouse. Half of the total land in the country is owned by 608 owners, while the eighteen largest landowners alone own 10 percent of Scotland. No other country in the west shows this level of inequality.

The tourism sector is vital to the Scottish economy, with over 14.6 million visitors to Scotland in 2015. Tourists from Great Britain make up the largest proportion of visitors. Most of the foreign visitors come from the United States, Germany, France, Australia, the Netherlands, and Canada. Scotland is generally seen as a clean and relatively unspoiled travel destination, with beautiful landscapes and a long and complex history, traced back to thousands of historical sites and attractions.

And what is haggis? Dr. Google cannot convey such a thing: It really tastes very good!

## Wales:

The western tip of Great Britain, it borders on England, the Celtic and Irish Seas; the capital is Cardiff (Caerdydd in Welsh). The country is counted among the six Celtic nations. The Welsh language is an important source of national identity for many Welsh people. It is still widely spoken, especially in the north, west and interior of the country. Historically, Welsh has become a minority language in the wake of the Industrial Revolution. Since 1993, the English and Welsh languages have been formally equalized. The bilingualism is particularly evident in the town and road signs. Since the 14$^{th}$ century, the titel "Prince of Wales" has traditionally - but not automatically - been that of the heir to the throne of most British monarchs, usually the eldest living son of the ruling British monarch (the Crown Prince). The current 21$^{st}$ Prince of Wales is Prince Charles, the eldest son of Queen Elizabeth II.

With 20,735 km², Wales is the smallest part of Great Britain. The coast is defined by cliffs and extensive beaches, over 1200 kilometers.

The interior is defined by the Cambrian Mountains, by extensive meadows, hilly landscapes, moors and mountains.

Large areas in Wales are protected biospheres. The highest mountains are the Snowdon (Yr Wyddfa, 1085 m), the Aran Fawddwy (905 m) and the Cadair Idris (893 m). There are three national parks in Wales: Snowdonia National Park, Brecon Beacons National Park and Pembrokeshire Coast National Park. Important rivers are the River Dee (Welsh Afon Dyfrdwy about 110 km) and the River Clwyd (55 km), which flow into Liverpool Bay. The River Teifi (117 km) as well as the Afon Tywi (120 km) and the River Wye (215 km) flow to the west.

Often cloudy, wet and windy, with warm summers and mild winters, Wales is considered one of the wettest countries in Europe. The climate on the southern coast is considerably milder than in the rest of the country due to warm ocean currents.

In the 18th and 19th centuries, Wales' mineral resources, such as coal, iron, copper, lime, shale, lead, tin, zinc and silver, made the region one of the most important places of the Industrial Revolution. In the second half of the 19th century, mining and metallurgy dominated the Welsh economy. From the mid-19th century to the mid-1980s, the mining and export of coal was a major endeavor: Cardiff was once the world's largest coal export port.

From the early 1970s, the Welsh economy underwent a massive restructuring, with large numbers of jobs lost in traditional heavy industry, which were replaced by new ones in lighter industry and the service sector.

## Facts for a direct comparison

### Germany
**area**: 357.582 km²
**extent**: The greatest north-south distance is 876 km, from east to west 640 km.
**residents**: 83.02 Million
**population density**: 233 inhabitants per km²
**capital**: Berlin with 3.7 Million residents

### Sweden
**area**: 447.435 km²
**extent**: The greatest north-south distance is 1572 km, from east to west 499 km.
**residents**: 10.23 Million

**population density**: 23 inhabitants per km²
**capital**: Stockholm with 975.904 residents

## Great Britain
**area**: 243.610 km²
**extent**: The greatest north-south distance is 970 km, from east to west 490 km.
**residents**: 66.4 Million
**population density**: 273 inhabitants per km²
**capital**: London with 8.9 Million residents

## England
**area**: 130.395 km²
**extent**: The greatest north-south distance is 630 km, from east to west 490 km.
**residents**: 55.9 Million
**population density**: 429 inhabitants per km²
**capital**: London with 8.9 Million residents

## Northern Ireland
**area**: 13.843 km²
**extent**: The greatest north-south distance is 140 km, from east to west 180 km.
**residents**: 1.8 Million
**population density**: 136 inhabitants per km²
**capital**: Belfast with 280.211 residents

## Republic of Ireland
**area**: 70.273 km²

**extent**: The greatest north-south distance is 485 km, from east to west 275 km.

**residents**: 4.7 Million

**population density**: 68 inhabitants per km²

**capital**: Dublin with 1.3 Million residents

## Scotland

**area**: 77.910 km²

**extent**: The greatest north-south distance is 440 km, from east to west 250 km.

**residents**: 5.4 Million

**population density**: 70 inhabitants per km²

**capital**: Edinburgh with 518.500 residents

## Wales

**area**: 20.735 km²

**extent:** The greatest north-south distance is 275 km, from east to west 100 km.

**residents**: 3.1 Million

**population density**: 151 inhabitants per km²

**capital**: Cardiff with 361.468 residents

© The Dünchem couple, thanks for the great photo!

## 10. Related Literature Tips by Anna Zoch

**For Sweden and Lapland:**
Jens Andersen: Astrid Lindgren: The Woman Behind Pippi Longstocking; Yale University Press, 2018; ISBN: 978-0300226102

Åsa Larsson: Until Thy Wrath be Past. Thriller, Verlag: Maclehose Press Quercus, 2014; ISBN: 978-1623651695

Ingrid Zellner: Malin and the White Reindeer: A story for children and grown-ups, Tredition Gmbh 2017; ISBN: 978-3743977297

Books by Astrid Lindgren

**For England, Scotland and Ireland:**
Anka Muhlstein: Elizabeth I and Mary Stuart: The Perils of Marriage. Haus Publishing Limited 2007; ISBN: 978-1904950851

Stefan Zweig: Mary Queen of Scots. Pushkin Press, 2018; ISBN 978-1782275459

Stefan Zweig: Mary Stuart. Kindel Edition, 2017

Heinrich Böll: Irish Journal, Melville House Publishing, 2011; ISBN 978-1935554196

**I do not claim this to be a complete list!**

# 11. Closing Words and a Thank You!

All of the experiences told here have actually happened in the past few years. I would like to thank my many travel guests for the beautiful and also strange moments that we have experienced together. Nothing is more exciting than traveling with people!

**„Sometimes the most beautiful things happen exactly when you don't expect them."**

I would particularly like to thank my parents Doris & Reiner Zoch and my friends and acquaintances Hiltrud Baier, Eva Lorenz, Rudolf & Cläre Schmitz, Cäcilie Thiemann for their constructive and mental support: many thanks to you all!

**A very special thank you to Maren Zimmermann for this translation, without you this book would not be possible!!**

Thank you so much „Tack så mycket" also to Helena Länta and Tor Moberg Heatta for their consent in regards to the photos with them and I would like to share with you the link to the shop of the Länta family in Jokkmokk:

**Sápmi Ren & Vilt AB,** Hantverkargatan 71, 962 33 Jokkmokk, Schweden; https://sapmirenovilt.se/

I am only responsible for the content. I apologize for any factual errors and thank you for any information and feedback: a.zoch@gmx.de

## Who is Anna Zoch?

 Anna Zoch is born in 1976 in Lower Saxonie and studied history and German at the University of Osnabrück with a "Magistra Atrium" degree (M.A.). Cathedral tours and museum education for the Diocese of Osnabrück were her first steps in tourism. For a tour operator from the Rhineland, she began her "journey" as a tour guide in 2005, and in 2011 she started her own business. Since then she has been working with great enthusiasm and very successfully, mainly in Scotland, Sweden, the Netherlands and soon also in Ireland for many well-known tour operators. She now lives in the Ruhr area in Germany.

# Information about the photos:

Front page: "Iron boy";  old town of Stockholm

p. 10: Karlskrona in southern Sweden

p. 21: Stockholm & Malmö in southern Sweden

p. 24/25: Gotha in Thuringia & Stockholm

p. 32: Urqhart Castle (Loch Ness) in Scotland

p. 38: Rannoch Moor & Drumnadrochit - Scotland

p. 44: Tobermory on the Isle of Mull in Scotland

p. 49: Glenfinnan in Scotland

p. 55: Eilean Donan Castle & Glen Coe in Scotland

p. 62 & 65: Braemar in Scotland

p. 68: Cliffs of Moher in Ireland

p. 77: Land's End in Cornwall, England

p. 86: Kiruna in swedish Lapland

p. 91: Vaimat bei Jokkmokk in swedish Lapland

p. 121: Scotland: Stirling & Scone Palace

p. 124: Skansen in Stockholm, Sweden

p. 126: Jokkmokk in swedish Lapland


All photos are mine, except one:
Many thanks to the Dünchem couple!

## As an encore, a photo from Lapland:

New Year's 2018/19 in Jokkmokk!
Photo shooting with Tor Moberg Heatta:
Mange takk, det var en superfin kveld med deg!